T0343493

Super Safari 3

Letters and Numbers Workbook

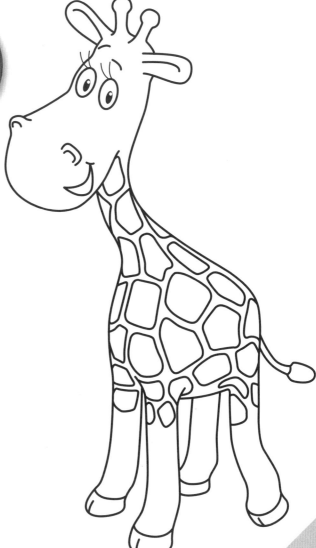

Color in Gina!

CAMBRIDGE
UNIVERSITY PRESS

Shaftesbury Road, Cambridge CB2 8EA, United Kingdom

One Liberty Plaza, 20th Floor, New York, NY 10006, USA

477 Williamstown Road, Port Melbourne, VIC 3207, Australia

314–321, 3rd Floor, Plot 3, Splendor Forum, Jasola District Centre, New Delhi – 110025, India

103 Penang Road, #05-06/07, Visioncrest Commercial, Singapore 238467

Cambridge University Press & Assessment is a department of the University of Cambridge.

We share the University's mission to contribute to society through the pursuit of education, learning and research at the highest international levels of excellence.

First published 2016

20 19 18 17 16 15 14 13

Printed in Poland by Opolgraf

ISBN 978-1-316-60952-1 Letters and Numbers Workbook 3

Additional resources for this publication at www.cambridge.org/supersafari

Cambridge University Press & Assessment has no responsibility for the persistence or accuracy of URLs for external or third-party internet websites referred to in this publication, and does not guarantee that any content on such websites is, or will remain, accurate or appropriate. Information regarding prices, travel timetables, and other factual information given in this work is correct at the time of first printing but Cambridge University Press & Assessment does not guarantee the accuracy of such information thereafter.

Super Safari 3

Letters and Numbers Workbook

Hello!

The children draw their face. Write each child's name with a gray pencil. The children trace their name with colored pencils.

1 Draw and trace.

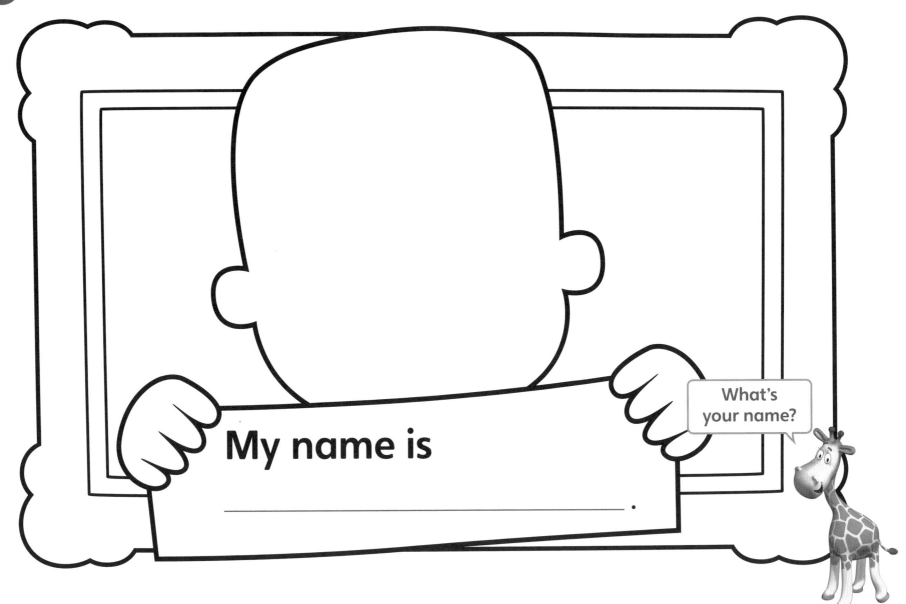

My name is

What's your name?

1 Connect the dots. Color the bag.

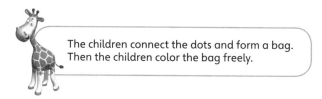

The children connect the dots and form a bag.
Then the children color the bag freely.

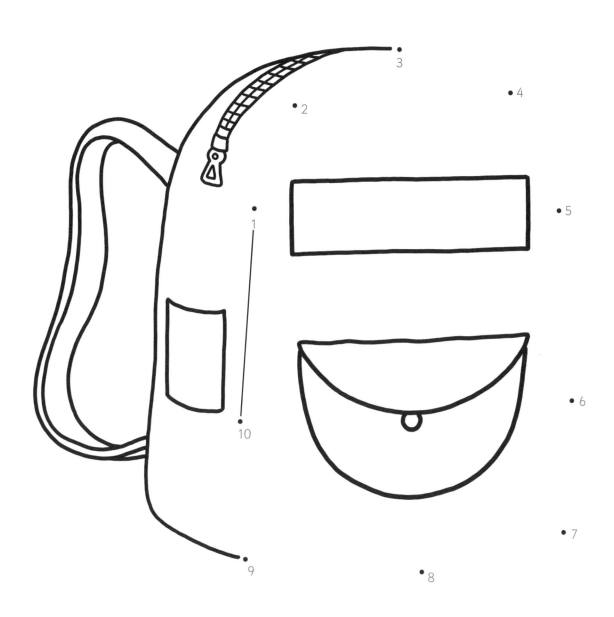

1 My classroom

1 Trace the letters.

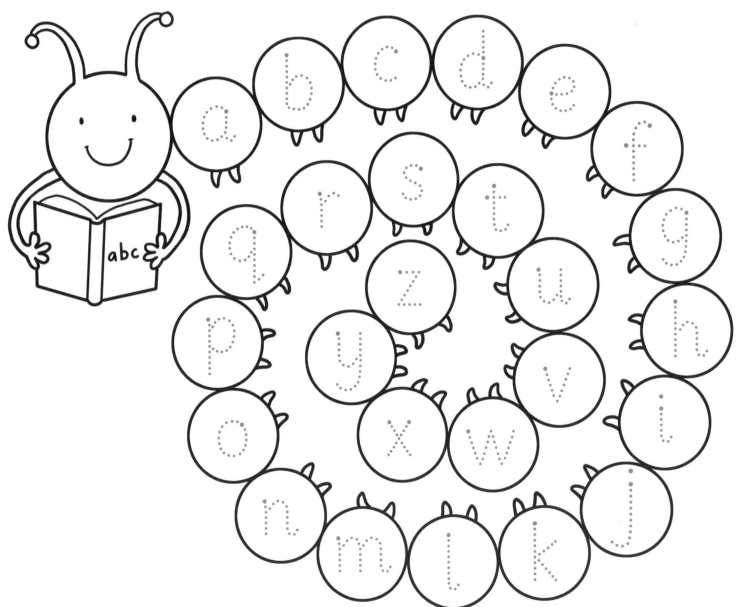

1 Count, circle, and color.

Review the numbers from 1 to 5. Next, the children count the objects in each box and circle the corresponding number. Finally, the children color the objects and numbers freely.

2 / 5   4 / 3   2 / 1

1 / 4   4 / 5   5 / 3

1 Look and match. Color the pictures.

Review the alphabet. Then the children look at the letters and match them with the corresponding pictures. Finally, the children color the pictures freely.

a c e g j m

1 **Color the correct number of objects.**

Review the numbers from 1 to 10. Then the children point to the number 9 and color nine crayons. Repeat the procedure for the remaining numbers and items.

9

8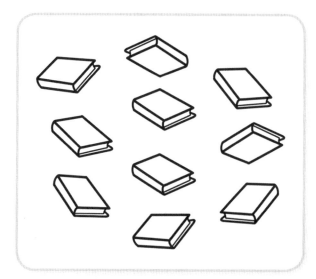

6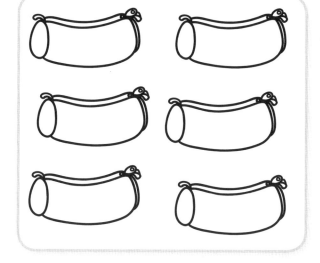

7

1 **Look, mark, and color.**

The children mark the letter each picture starts with. Finally, they color in the pictures freely.

	n	j	f	l
(nest)	☐	☐	☐	☐

	d	t	r	q
(queen)	☐	☐	☐	☐

	w	x	v	y
(xylophone)	☐	☐	☐	☐

	b	s	z	k
(zebra)	☐	☐	☐	☐

1 Write the missing numbers. Color.

Review the numbers from 1 to 10. Then the children look at the first series of numbers and write the missing number. Repeat the procedure for the remaining series. Finally, the children color the pictures freely.

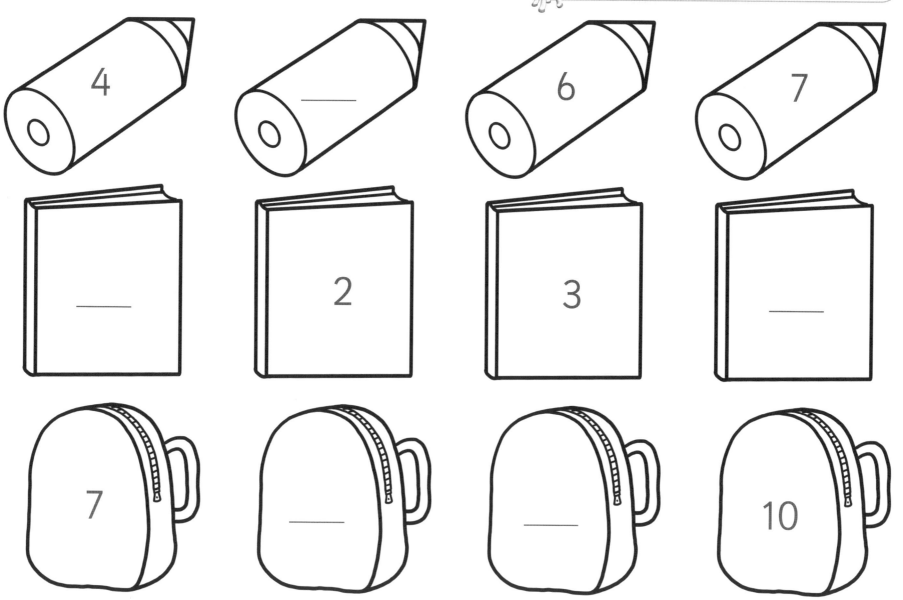

4   ___   6   7

___   2   3   ___

7   ___   ___   10

1 **Listen and match. Color the pictures.**

Say /r/ – /r/ – /r/ – *rabbit*. Repeat with *red*. Next, ask *Does rope begin with the /r/ sound? Yes!* The children match *rope* with the letter "r". Continue in the same manner with the rest of the activity. Finally, the children color the pictures freely.

rope

ring

rainbow

robot

1 Color, glue, and cut. Play.

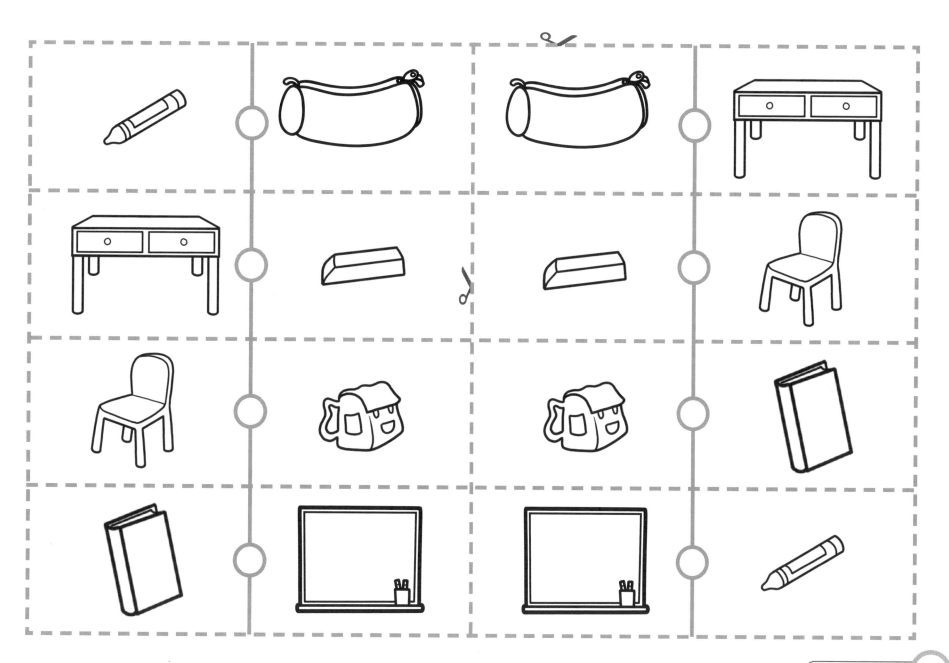

Color, glue, and cut. Play.

Materials:
piece of construction paper, glue, scissors, colored pencils

Instructions:
The children identify the classroom objects and color them. Next, they glue the page onto a piece of construction paper. Once dry, the children cut out the dominoes and play on their own or with a partner.

1 **Listen. Color the pictures.**

Say *The chair is blue*. The children color the chair blue. Repeat the procedure for the following items: pencil-yellow, eraser-red, book-green, bag-orange, desk-purple.

2 My family

The children identify the family members. Then the children trace the words with colored pencils. Finally, the children color the pictures freely.

1 Trace. Color the pictures.

grandpa

grandma

dad

mom

sister

brother

1 Connect the dots. Color the house.

Review the numbers from 1 to 20. Say *Families live in houses.* Next, the children connect the dots. Ask *What is it? A house!* Finally, the children color the house freely.

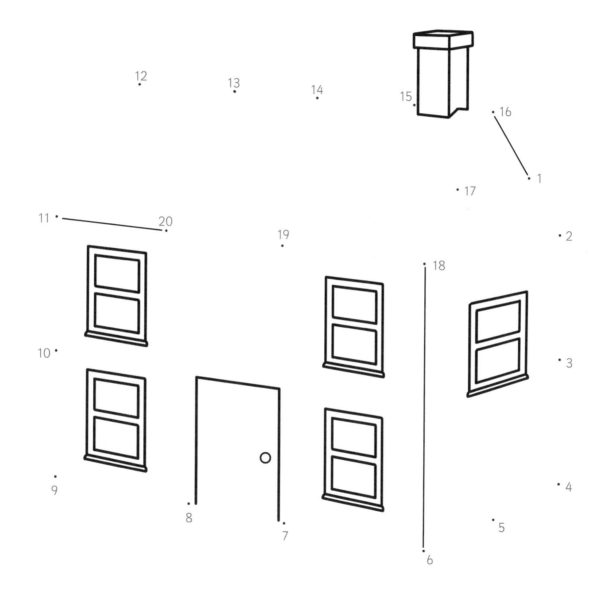

1 Trace. Color the correct frame.

The children trace the words with colored pencils. Then they color the corresponding frames.

This is my grandpa.

This is my grandma.

This is my dad.

1 **Count and match. Color the pictures.**

Review the numbers from 1 to 20. Then the children count the dots on each tie. Next, they match the ties with the corresponding numbers. Finally, the children color the pictures freely.

10   4   14   20

1 **Trace and match. Color.**

The children trace the words with colored pencils. Then the children match the sentences with the corresponding pictures. Finally, the children color the pictures freely.

This is my mom.

This is my sister.

This is my brother.

1 Count. Write the numbers.

 Review the numbers from 10 to 20. Then the children count the objects in each box and write the corresponding number on the lines.

_____

_____

_____

_____

_____

_____

1 **Listen and trace. Color the pictures.**

Say /f/ – /f/ – /f/ – *fish*, *family*. Then the children trace the letter "f" in each word. Next, they say each word aloud. Finally, the children color the pictures freely.

f an

f lower

f oot

f ox

f ork

f rog

1 Make and assemble a puzzle.

Make and assemble a puzzle.

Materials:
construction paper, glue, colored pencils, scissors

Instructions:
The children color the scene. Then they glue the page onto a piece of construction paper. Next, they cut out the scene along the dotted lines to make puzzle pieces. Finally, the children assemble the puzzle.

1 **Read and circle. Color the pictures.**

The children look at the pictures and circle the correct words. Then they color the pictures freely.

dad / mom

sister / brother

grandma / grandpa

dad / mom

grandpa / brother

sister / grandpa

3 My face

1 Follow, match, and trace. Color.

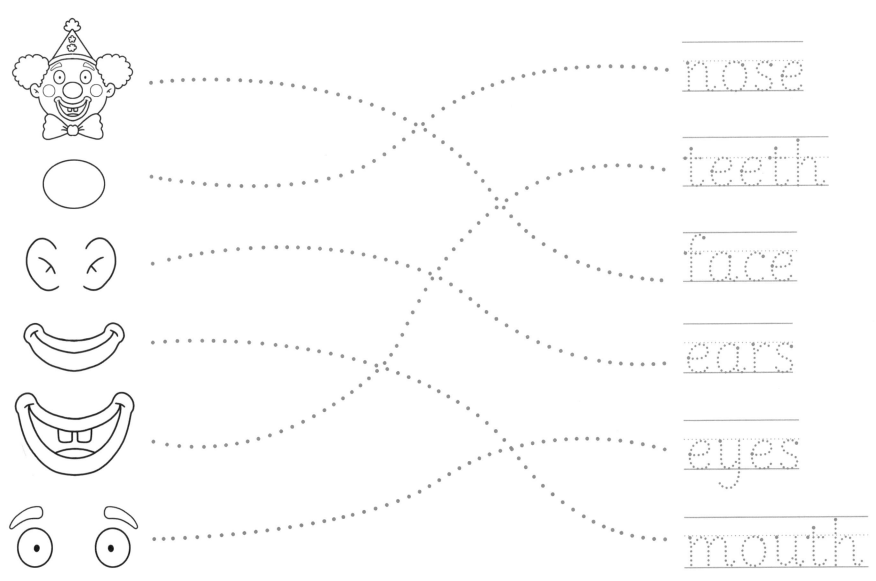

nose

teeth

face

ears

eyes

mouth

1 Count and color the numbers.

Present the numbers. The children count the mouths and ears in each box. Next, the children color the numbers freely.

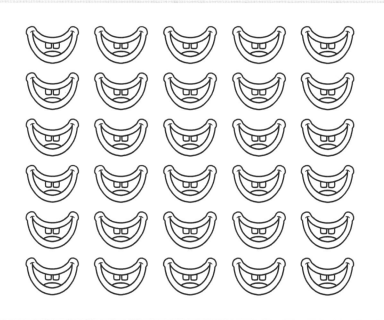

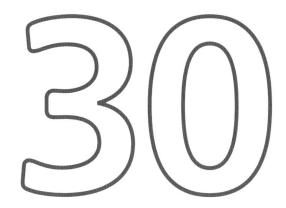

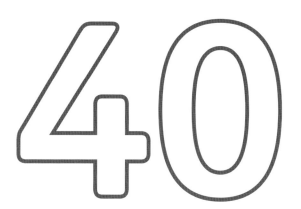

1 **Trace and match. Color the pictures.**

The children trace the words with colored pencils.
Next, the children match the sentences with the corresponding pictures.
Finally, the children color the pictures freely.

This is my mouth.

This is my nose.

This is my face.

1 **Count and circle the correct number.**

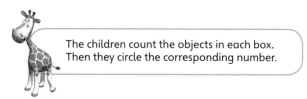

The children count the objects in each box. Then they circle the corresponding number.

30 / 40   30 / 40

1 **Trace. Circle the correct picture.**

The children trace the words with colored pencils. Next, the children circle the correct pictures. Finally, the children color the pictures they circled.

They're my *eyes.*

They're my *ears.*

 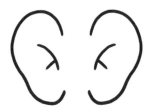

They're my *teeth.*

1 **Draw five more.**

The children count the objects in each box. Then they draw five more to complete the objects needed.

= **30**

= **40**

1 **Listen and write. Color the pictures.**

Say /h/ – /h/ – /h/ – *hat, happy. Does hen begin with the /h/ sound? Yes!* Next, the children write a letter "h" at the beginning of *hen*. Repeat for *house* and *hand*. Finally, the children color the pictures freely.

___en

___ouse

___and

1 Color the faces. Cut out and assemble.

I am

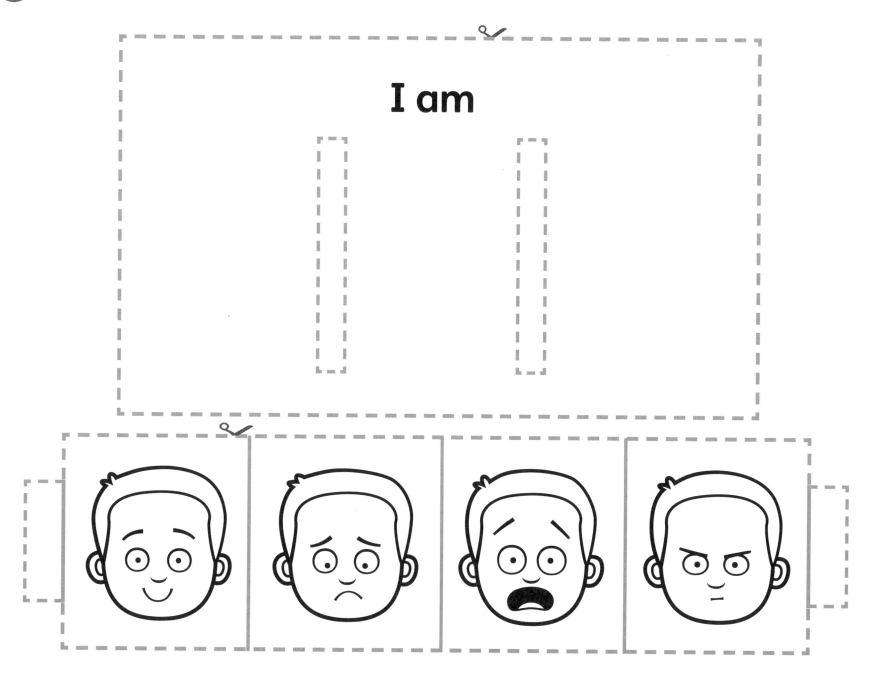

Color the faces. Cut out and assemble.

Materials:

scissors, crayons, glue

Instructions:

The children color the faces. Next, they cut out the slits and make two slots. Help the children insert the strip through the slots and pull on it from side to side to move the faces. Finally, the children say how they feel.

1 **Read and match. Color the picture.**

The children match the words with the corresponding pictures. Then the children color the clown's face freely.

eyes

face

ears

teeth

nose

mouth

4 My toys

The children write the words in the boxes.
Then the children color the toys freely.

1 Write. Color the toys.

plane jump rope kite doll ball

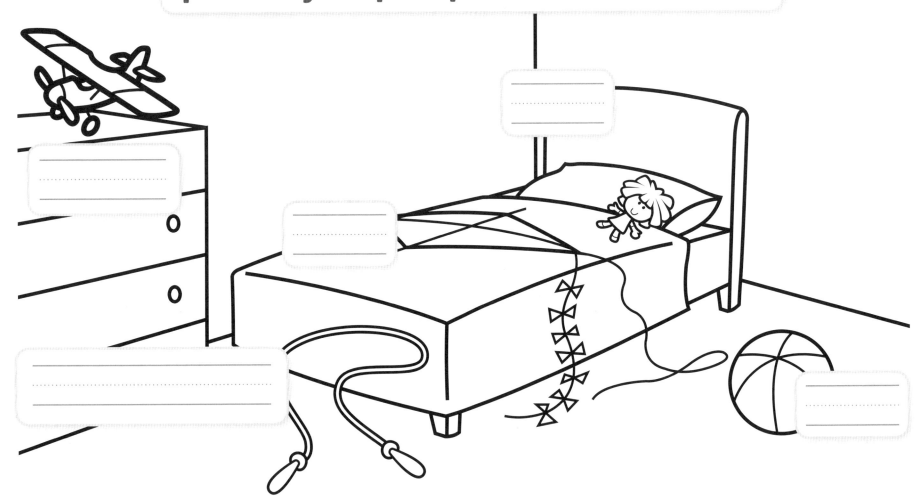

1 **Count and match. Color the numbers.**

The children count the toys in each box and match the boxes with the corresponding numbers. Then the children color the numbers freely.

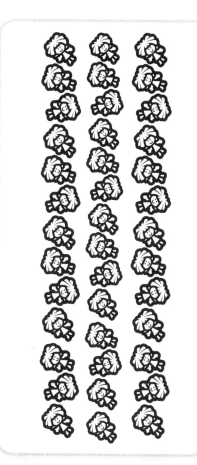
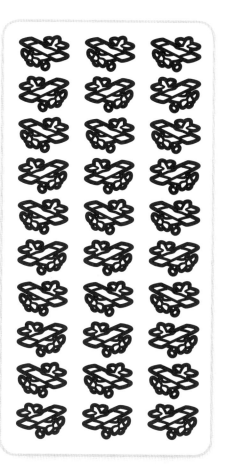

30 40 10 20

1 **Circle and write. Color the pictures.**

doll   teddy bear

I have a _____.

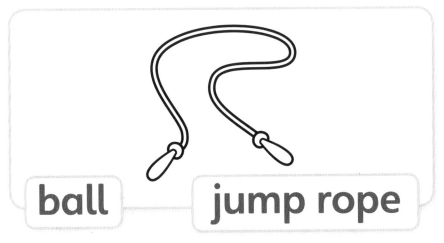

ball   jump rope

I have a _____.

plane   kite

I have a _____.

1 Count and circle.

The children count the toys in each box. Then they circle the corresponding number.

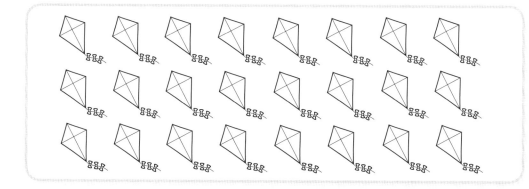

20/24

33/35

29/40

1 **Mark the correct word. Write.**

We have a _____.

☐ jump rope   ☐ kite

We have a _____.

☐ ball   ☐ plane

We have a _____.

☐ teddy bear   ☐ doll

1 Write the missing numbers. Color

The children complete the two series of numbers. Then they color the pictures freely.

Bears: ___ 36 ___ 38

Kites: 43 ___ 45 ___

1 **Listen. Color the correct pictures.**

Say /g/ – /g/ – /g/ – dog, dig. Color the pictures that end with the /g/ sound. Does bag end with the /g/ sound? Yes! Then the children color the picture of the bag. Continue in the same manner with the rest of the activity.

ba_g_

ba_t_

fla_g_

fi_sh_

bu_g_

wi_n_

1 Color, cut out, and glue. Assemble.

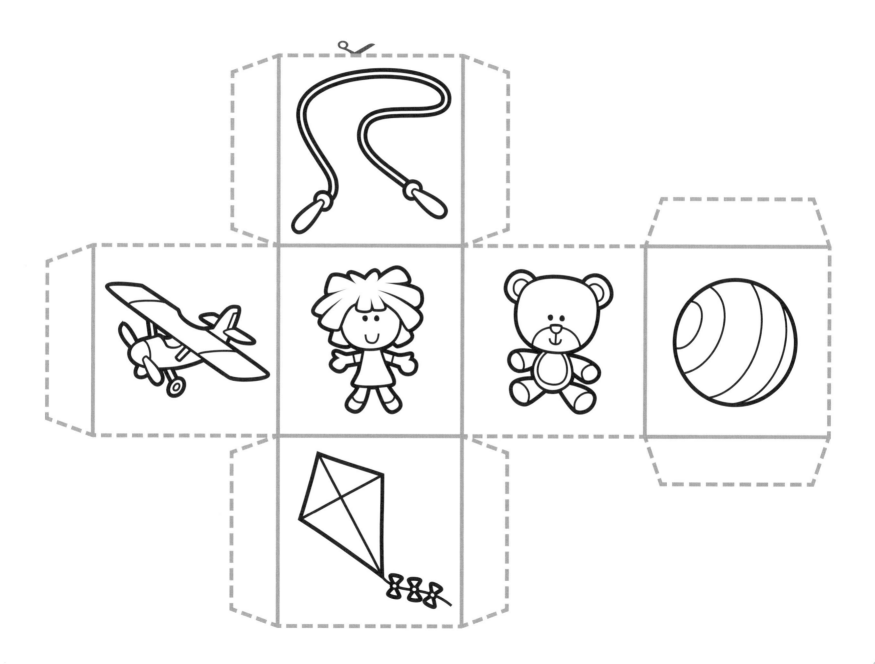

Color, cut out, and glue. Assemble.

Materials:

scissors, colored pencils, glue

Instructions:

The children color the pictures. Then they cut out the cube and assemble it. Then pair the children. The children take turns rolling the cubes and identifying the toys.

1 **Read. Color the correct picture.**

Read the word *plane*. The children read along. Then the children look at the pictures and color the one that depicts a toy plane. Repeat the procedure for the remaining words and pictures.

plane

teddy bear

doll

jump rope

5 My house

The children copy the words onto the lines. Then the children color the pictures freely.

1 Write. Color the pictures.

bathtub

_____
. . . .
_____

cabinet

_____
. . . .
_____

bed

_____
. . . .
_____

1 **Count and color.**

Present the number 50. The children count the petals in each flower. Finally, the children color the flowers freely.

10

20

30

40

50

1 **Trace, write, and color.**

The children trace the wavy lines from the pictures to the words. Then the children copy the words onto the lines. Finally, the children color the pictures freely.

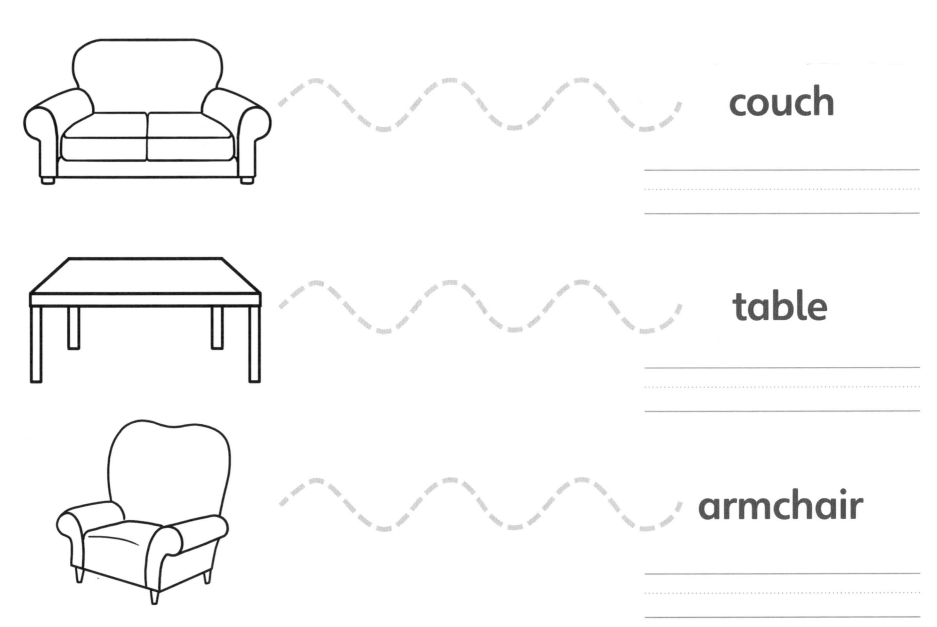

couch

table

armchair

Count and color.

1 **Write. Color the pictures.**

The children copy the words *cabinet*, *bed*, and *table* onto the lines to complete each sentence. Then they color the pictures freely.

cabinet

The ball is in the _____.

bed

The kite is on the _____.

table

The doll is under the _____.

1 Count. Circle the correct number.

The children count the kites and circle the correct number. Repeat the procedure for the armchairs.

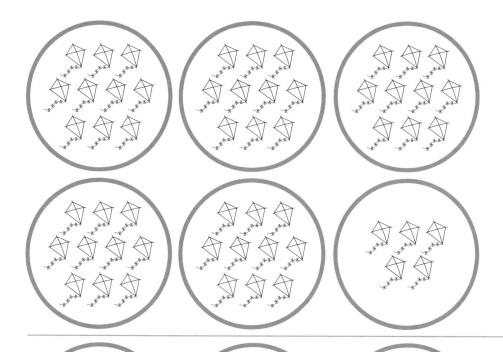

= **55   53   60**

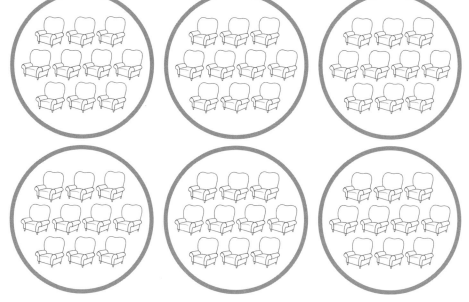

= **58   60   57**

1 **Listen, write, and color.**

Say /y/ – /y/ – /y/ – yogurt - yellow. Does yarn begin with the /y/ sound? Yes! Write the letter "y" on the lines to complete the word yarn. Then say Does jacket begin with the /y/ sound? No! Do not write the letter "y". Continue in the same manner with the rest of the activity. Next, the children read aloud the words that begin with the /y/ sound: yarn, yawn, yak. Finally, the children color only the pictures that begin with the /y/ sound.

_____ arn

_____ acket

_____ awn

_____ ar

_____ ak

1 Cut out and play.

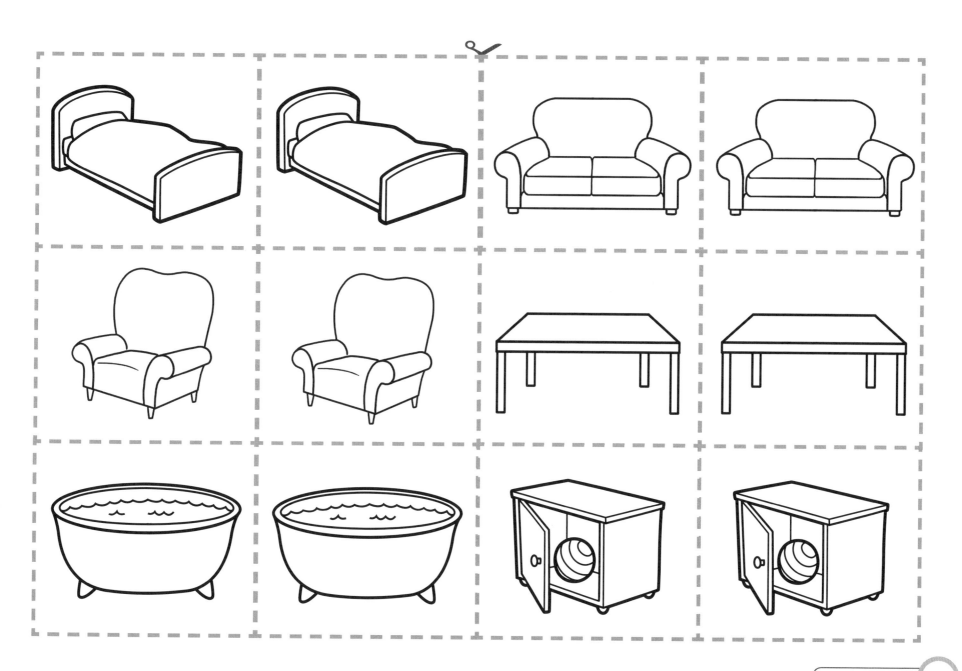

Cut out and play.

Materials:

scissors, colored pencils, glue, piece of construction paper (1 per child)

Instructions:

The children color the furniture items in each box. Then they detach the page and glue it onto a piece of construction paper. Once dry, the children cut out the boxes to make memory cards. The children shuffle the cards. Then they put the cards face down in rows on a table. The children turn over two cards. If the cards match, the children put them aside. If they do not match, the children turn them back over. The children continue playing until all the matching cards are found.

1 **Complete, circle, and color.**

The children look at the pictures and complete them. Then they circle the correct word. Finally, the children color the pictures freely.

couch / table

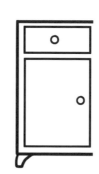

bed / cabinet

armchair / bed

couch / bathtub

table / bed

cabinet / couch

6 On the farm

The children trace the sentences. Next, the children draw and color the animals' missing parts. Finally, the children color the animals freely.

1 Trace. Draw the missing parts. Color.

This is a cat.

This is a horse.

This is a dog.

1 **Count. Paint the number.**

Present the number. Next, the children count the sheep by tens. Finally, the children paint the number 70 with watercolors.

1 Trace, match, and color.

The children trace the sentences with colored pencils. Next, the children match the sentences to the corresponding pictures. Finally, the children color the pictures freely.

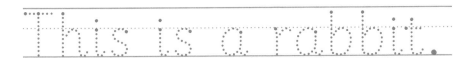

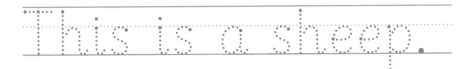

1 **Count and color.**

Present the number. Next, the children count the dots on the butterflies in sets of ten. Finally, the children color the dots on each butterfly freely.

80

1 **Trace and draw.**

The children trace the sentences. Then the children illustrate each sentence.

I like cats.

I like dogs.

I like horses.

1 **Connect the dots. Color the rabbit.**

Review the numbers from 1 to 80. Then the children connect the dots and form a rabbit. Finally, the children color the rabbit freely.

1 Listen, match, and color.

Say /z/ – /z/ – /z/ – zebra-zoo. Ask Does zipper start with the /z/ sound? Yes! Match zipper with the letter "z". Continue in the same manner with the rest of the activity. Finally, the children color the pictures freely.

zipper

z

zigzag

zero

zeppelin

1 Make finger puppets.

Make finger puppets.

Materials:
colored crayons, scissors, tape

Instructions:
The children color each animal. Next, the children cut out the animals. Help the children join the ends of the tabs with tape. Make sure the puppets adjust to the children's fingers. Finally, the children play with their finger puppets.

1 **Color the farm animals. Match.**

The children color the farm animals. Next, the children match the pictures to the corresponding words.

cat

horse

cow

dog

rabbit

sheep

7 I'm hungry!

The children trace the sentences and mark the correct pictures. Next, the children color the pictures they marked.

1 Trace, mark, and color.

I like carrots.

 ☐  ☐

I like apples.

 ☐  ☐

I like cake.

 ☐  ☐

1 Count and write the number.

The children identify and count the cakes. Then they write the total number of cakes on the line. Repeat the same procedure for the remaining food items. Finally, the children color the pictures freely.

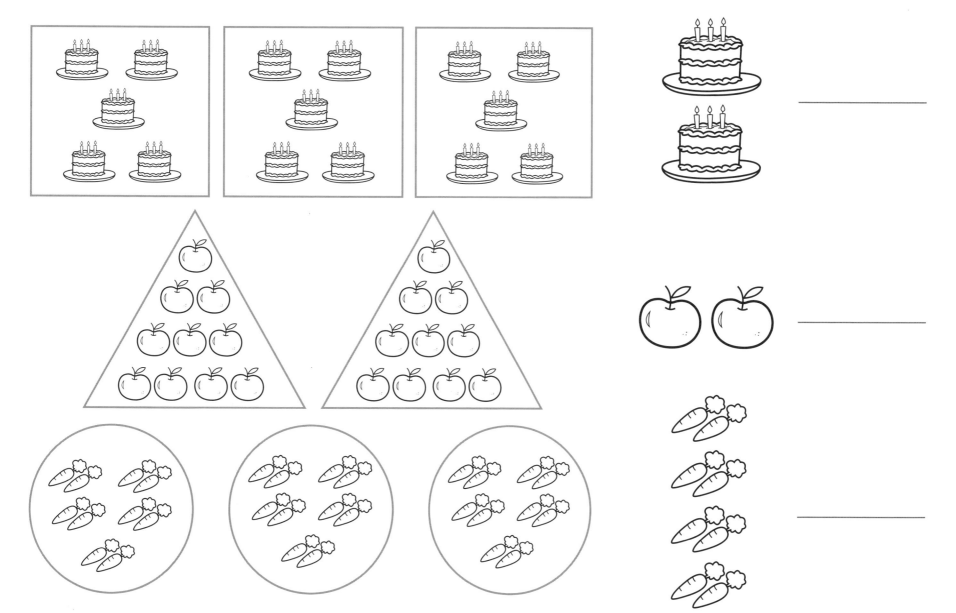

1 **Trace. Cross out the correct picture.**

The children trace the sentences. Next, the children cross out the corresponding picture. Finally, the children color the pictures they crossed out.

I don't like sausages.

I don't like ice cream.

I don't like fries.

1 **Count, write, and color.**

The children count the food items in each box. Then they write the corresponding amount of food items next to each picture. Finally, the children color the apple, the sausage, and the carrot freely.

How many?

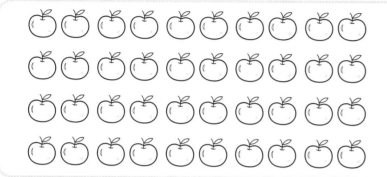

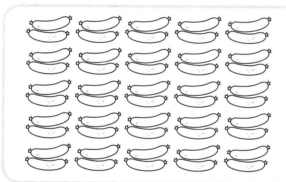

1 **Trace. Circle and color the correct picture.**

I like apples.

I don't like cake.

I don't like ice cream.

I don't like sausages.

1 **Write the missing numbers. Color.**

Review the numbers from 10 to 80. Next, the children look at the picture and write the missing numbers. Finally, the children color the picture freely.

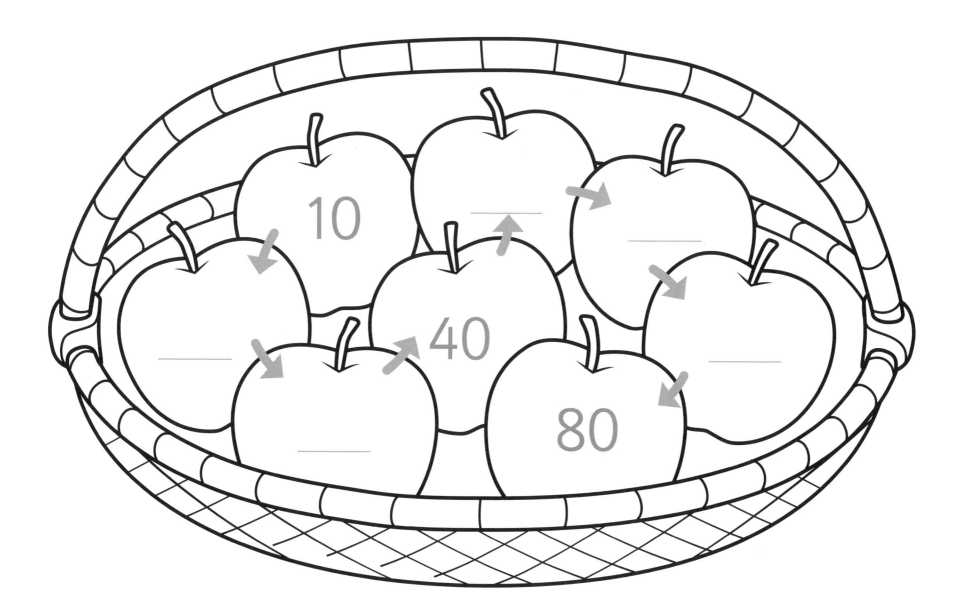

1 **Listen, match, and color.**

Say /k/ – /k/ – /k/ – cat – king. Next, say the words car, kite, cap, key, and koala. Next, the children match the pictures to the corresponding words. Then the children find the letter "c" or "k" in each word. Finally, the children color the pictures freely.

c   k

koala

car

key

cap

kite

1 **Color and cut out. Sort.**

I like

I don't like

Color and cut out. Sort.

Materials:
colored pencils, scissors, glue

Instructions:
The children identify the food items and color them.
Next, they cut them out. The children glue the food
items onto the corresponding column,
depending on whether they like them
or not.

1 **Circle the correct word. Color.**

The children look at the patterns and identify the food items. Then the children circle the word that comes next in each pattern.

 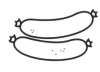   **carrots / apples**

     **sausages / fries**

     **carrots / cake**

 **apples / sausages**

    **ice cream / fries**

8 All aboard!

The children copy the sentences onto the lines. Next, the children color the pictures freely.

1 Read and write. Color the pictures.

I'm riding a bike.

I'm riding a scooter.

I'm driving a car.

1 **Count and color.**

Present the number. Next, the children count the planes in sets of ten. Finally, the children color the number 90.

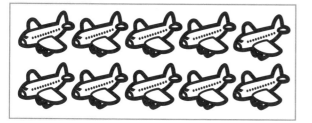

1 **Circle, write, and color.**

The children circle the correct pictures. Then the children copy the sentences onto the lines. Finally, the children color the pictures freely.

You're flying a plane.

You're sailing a boat.

1 **Count. Color the number.**

Present the number. The children count the windows on the buses in sets of ten. Then they color the number 100 freely.

 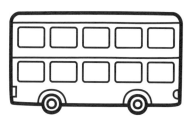  

 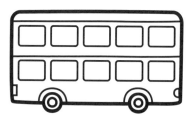  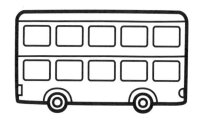

100

1 **Mark, write and color.**

The children look at the pictures. Then they mark the correct speech bubbles. Next, they copy the corresponding sentences onto the lines. Finally, they color the pictures freely.

I'm driving a train.

I'm driving a bus.

I'm riding a bike.

I'm sailing a boat.

1 Count. Circle the correct number.

Review the numbers from 10 to 100. Then the children count the stars on the sailboats and circle the corresponding number. Repeat the procedure for the windows on the buses.

How many?

90   95   93

100   90   95

1 **Listen and trace. Color the pictures.**

Say /ŋ/ – /ŋ/ – /ŋ/ – *dancing- singing, running, riding,* and *sailing.* Next, the children connect the letters and trace the arrows from the letters to the words and from the words to the pictures. Then the children identify the letters "n" and "g" at the end of each word and trace them. Finally, the children color the pictures freely.

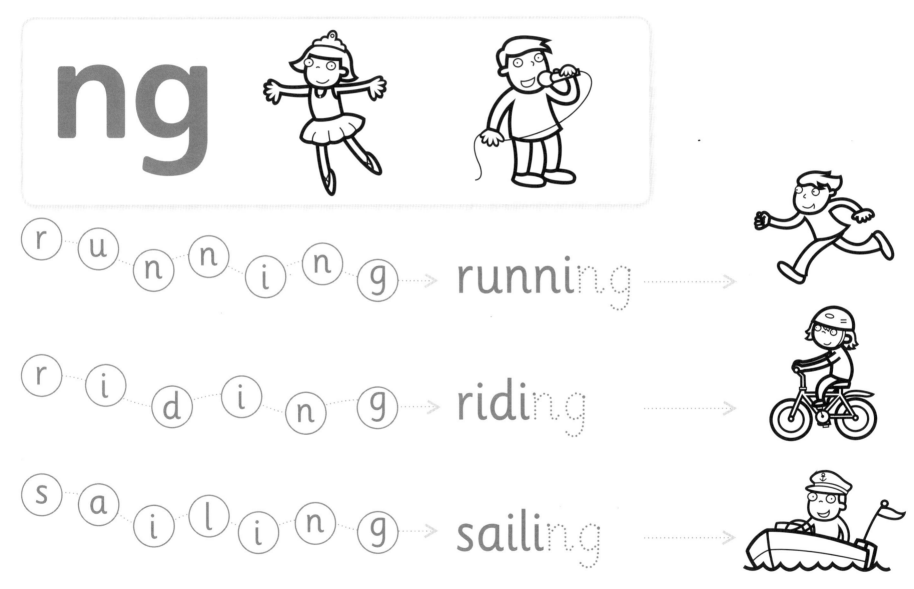

ng

r u n n i n g → running →

r i d i n g → riding →

s a i l i n g → sailing →

1 Paint and cut out. Glue and assemble.

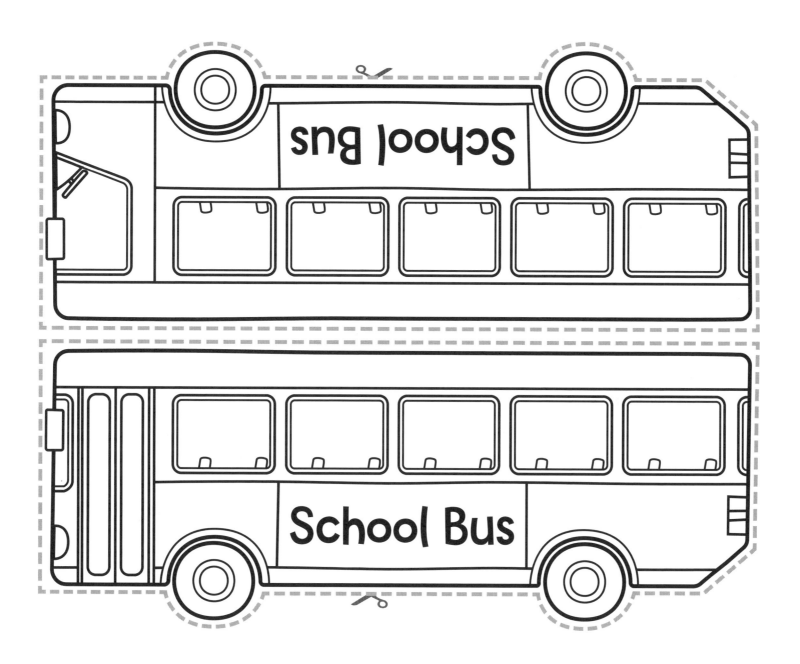

School Bus

Paint and cut out. Glue and assemble.

Materials:

yellow and black tempera paint, paintbrush
(1 per child), scissors, glue, tissue box (1 per child)

Instructions:

The children paint the school bus yellow and the
wheels black. Then they paint the tissue box yellow.
Once dry, the children cut out the school
bus and glue one part onto each side of
their box.

1 **Solve the puzzle.**

The children look at the pictures and identify the means of transportation. Then the children solve the puzzle.

1	
2	

```
Across →

2.        3.        5.
```

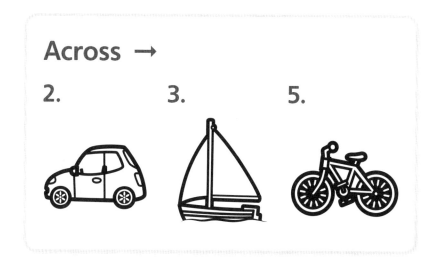

```
Down ↓

1.        4.        5.
```

9 Party clothes

The children copy the words *I like your* onto the first line and complete the sentence with the word *boots*. Repeat the procedure for the remaining items. Finally, the children color the pictures freely.

1 Read, write, and color.

I like your hat.

boots

shoes

buttons

1 Write the missing numbers. Color.

Review the numbers from 10 to 100. Next, the children write the missing numbers on the path with colored pencils. Finally, the children color the picture freely.

1 Look, write, and color.

The children copy the words *He has a* and complete the sentence with the words *red* and *hat*. Repeat the procedure for the remaining sentences. Finally, the children color the pictures freely.

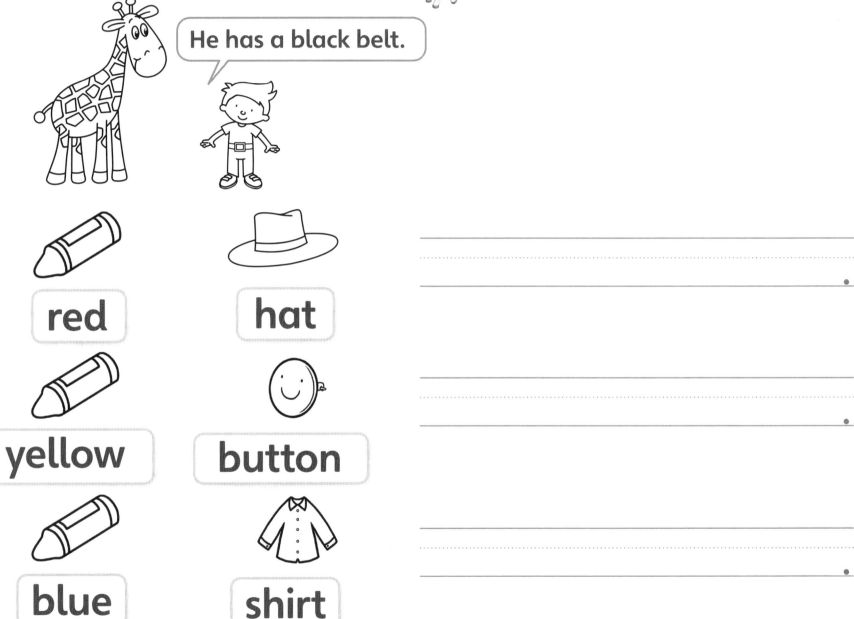

He has a black belt.

red   hat

yellow   button

blue   shirt

1 **Trace. Color the numbers.**

Review the numbers from 10 to 100. Then the children identify the number 10, trace a line from the number 10 to the number 20 and so on, using a colored pencil. Finally, the children color the numbers freely.

10

70

20

80

60

30

90

50

40

100

1 Trace and write. Color the pictures.

The children trace the arrows and connect the words to form sentences. Then they copy the sentences onto the lines. Finally, the children color the pictures freely.

Let's → have → ice cream

Let's → have → sausages

Let's → have → fries

1 Count. Cross out the extra objects.

Say *There are twenty-two hats. We only need twenty hats. Cross out the extra hats.* The children cross out two hats. Repeat the procedure for the remaining objects.

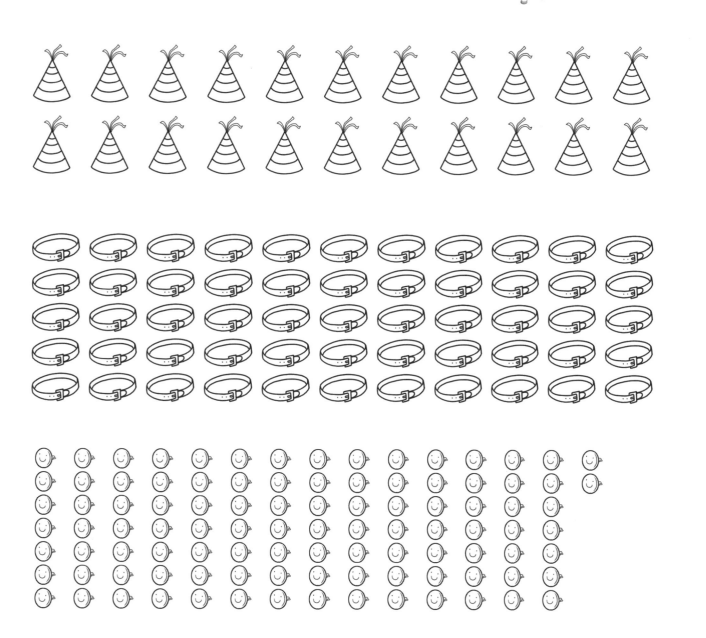

20

53

97

1 **Circle the correct letter. Color.**

Review the alphabet. Then the children look at the pictures and identify the objects. Next, the children circle the letter each word begins with.

a   i

c   k

j   h

u   w

k   q

m   n

s   c

x   y

z   x

1 Color and cut out. Dress the doll.

Color and cut out. Dress the doll.

Materials:
piece of construction paper (1 per child), scissors, glue, colored pencils

Instructions:
The children color the doll and the clothing items. Then they glue the doll onto a piece of construction paper. Once dry, the children cut out the doll and the clothing items. Finally, the children glue the clothes onto the doll.

1 Match. Color the pictures.

 The children match the letters to the corresponding lines in order to complete the words. Next, the children color the items freely.

s__i____

b__t__o__

__o__t__

__h_____s

Thanks and acknowledgements

The publishers are grateful to the following contributors:

Blooberry Design: cover design, book design, publishing management
and page make-up
Bill Bolton: cover illustration

The publishers and authors are grateful to the following illustrators:

Bill Bolton 1, 4, 86, 87, (1 and repeats on all pages of Gina);
Louise Gardner 5, 6, 7, 8, 9, 11, 13, 17, 21, 26, 27, 28, 29, 31, 35, 48, 52, 55,
61, 63, 65, 70, 86, 87, 88, 91, 92, 95; Marek Jagucki 4, 15, 16, 18, 19, 20,
23, 25, 33, 37, 38, 43, 45, 47, 50, 57, 58, 59, 67, 68, 69, 71, 73, 75, 78, 79, 80,
81, 83, 85, 93; Bernice Lum 8, 10, 12, 21, 22, 32, 36, 38, 39, 40, 41, 42, 45,
46, 49, 51, 52, 53, 56, 58, 62, 66, 67, 68, 69, 72, 73, 75, 76, 77, 82, 88, 90, 92